WALKING WITH GRACE
A LIFE JOURNEY THAT NEVER ENDS

WALKING WITH GRACE: A LIFE JOURNEY THAT NEVER ENDS

SPIRITUAL AFFIRMATION BOOK 2

CHARMAINE HOLLAND

Roses
ARE
RED
PUBLISHING

ISBN-13: 978-1-955265-13-3

Distributed by Roses Are Red Publishing
rosesareredpublishing.com

❀ Created with Vellum

BOOKS IN THE SPIRITUAL
AFFIRMATION SERIES

KEEP WALKING!

Dear Reader, thanks for reading. Let's stay in touch!

Visit me on my website at www.charmaineholland.com
Email me at hollandbook@gmail.com
Follow me on Facebook: https://www.facebook.com/charmainne.hollannd
Sign up for my newsletter, The Love of Inspiring Women here: https://eepurl.com/gGTV-P

Stepping into the Spiritual World of your Greatness

To my family, friends, and all whom I have desired to assist in discovering their best versions of themselves.

To all the individuals who have ever quietly dreamed of becoming someone or doing something significant with their lives but could not believe it was possible.

To the silent dreamer with a passion for greatness, who suffers from the intimidation of his/her culture and social surroundings.

To the aspiring and developing leader within each of us. May we all discover our greatness.

To all the great leaders who have truly been an inspiration in my life, I thank you.

Love Charmaine

AUTHOR'S NOTE

Author's Note

Walking In Grace is what I strive for each day that I'm given another chance. Every day, we are given an opportunity to expand by collecting our thoughts and the information we have gathered along the way. I stand in grace as I share my words of inspiration intended to offer guidance and strength and help me stand tall when the days seem challenging and I'm not sure which direction to turn. Only by God's grace and mercy am I led on this journey onto a path that's obscured at times, but always heads toward the right direction and helps me see the greater lessons in life.

Now, I understand that we're able to gain so much out of life if we focus on what we can, and not what we can't do. I hope this book of affirmations helps you as it helped me understand life on many levels while expanding my heart and mind to achieve so much more in life.

Sending Love and Light Your Way,
Charmaine Holland

INTRODUCTION

It's the emptiness of an unfamiliar space that we are often eager to fill with our heart's desires. We often wish to have better health, happiness, financial security, or peace of mind, so that we can embody the true expression of life. But many fail to achieve this goal, based on defining results.

What we see as true is just a notion that we overheard, not something that we truly believe. Without the right mindset to see things from a different perspective, we're left uncertain of what we truly desire. What we think is what we normally believe.

How we feel is what we normally accept without realizing that the feelings are only temporary and can be changed based on the perception of what we want and desire at that time in our life, for the most part.

Affirmations play a major part in what we say, think, and how to feel. By believing in what you say, whether it's good or bad, you're giving it a command.

We must speak life into our consciousness, so we can evolve ourselves into the next dimension. We have all heard the phrase a thousand times, that words are spells. Therefore, we must speak life into our very own existence, if we want to become what we say and what we focus on the most. For every word we speak, there's a command that takes place that forms into something concrete that affects our mind, body, and spirit. Grace is about giving yourself the free will to navigate within certain boundaries where you're able to enjoy life as you see fit.

This is what makes affirmations so special to each individual, because you are making commands and validating from within the spiritual realms. That helps guide you into this natural space, based on your belief system, and results in manifesting something beautiful into your natural born reality.

AFFIRMATION OF EMPOWERMENT

There's nothing that I can't do, once I believe I can do it.

Affirmation

- I have all the tools I need to be great!
- My mind is sharp like a pencil.
- My thinking capacity allows me to reach the highest mountains.

EMPOWERMENT

Empowerment requires lots of work and dedication. This is something that doesn't spring up for a person overnight. Empowerment develops over time and is a result of how you think. I have learned that empowerment is a combination of several other components that contribute to helping you reach a level of feeling empowered.

Let me explain. If someone is feeling down and needing someone to uplift them with words of encouragement, there must be a particular individual who has a certain amount of compassion and unconditional love to uplift humanity. We all know and understand that everything that we do is a part of a process toward reaching anything good in our lives.

AFFIRMATION OF DECISIONS

Not a day goes by that we don't have to make a decision that affects our lives.

Affirmation

- It's important to make conscious decisions all of the time.
- My decisions determine my future.
- If I can't see it, I can't achieve it.

DECISIONS

Many people are afraid of making decisions. What are decisions? Changes that affect the outcome of anything we do or say. Can I trust that the decisions that I make will have a major impact on my life that's worth making? Absolutely!!

Each question, each thought that crosses our mind, is a conscious thought that we must make every time we have to make a decision. Sometimes, we make decisions that we are unsure of, and we don't know what to expect from those decisions afterward. I just know and understand that each decision we make in life allows us to do one of three things: Move forward to make our life better, or take another route to prolong the process due to fear, or make no decision and stay stuck in the space called comfort zone. At the end of the day, we all want better, so we can become greater.

AFFIRMATION OF BUSINESS SUCCESS

To be a businessperson, you must have the right attitude and mindset if you want to become successful!

Affirmation

- I am successful.
- I create wealth daily.
- I create opportunities for others.

BUSINESS SUCCESS

Growing up, I always had a mindset that I was going to be successful by building an enterprise to leave behind for my children. I didn't know what would be required. I just knew that I didn't want to struggle all my life, like my parents. I wanted to teach and leave behind a business for my kids.

My mother had seven children. All my life, I watched her work. She never had time for herself, except for her days off from work. I thought by being a businesswoman, you could develop opportunity for time for yourself. This is true, but work and planning are endless when you are a businesswoman. It's the little things we learn along the way.

Whether you are a businesswoman for someone or yourself, if you want to be successful, it requires a lot of your personal time. You begin to work just to become successful. It's all about living comfortably and having nice things in life for the time and energy that you invest in your business or working for someone else. The real question is, do you want to work for someone else, which provides only an expiration date? Or would you prefer to love what you do for yourself by helping others become successful with your knowledge, guidance and support as you continue fulfilling your life purpose by spreading your wisdom among generation after generation?

AFFIRMATION OF ACHIEVEMENT

I'm unstoppable once I put my mind toward getting the job done.

Affirmation

- I'm a great achiever.
- I experience success with everything I touch and do.
- I'm unstoppable at every given moment.

ACHIEVEMENT

Anyone can strive toward excellence and experience great achievement. Some people take decades to reach achievement. It depends on a person's individual goals and dreams. Once we begin to achieve the things in life we desire, it becomes our normal state of being to constantly strive to achieve, especially when we have the right mindset.

I highly recommend always being practical about reaching your goals. Set small goals that are reachable in a short time frame. You can gain so much out of life if you focus on what you can do and not what you can't do.

I have learned that life will present certain tasks that require assistance from others. If you're not ready or they're not ready, it will leave you thinking, how did I get here? One thing I have learned is that we can't be successful on our own.

When you begin to understand what achievement can do for you, you'll start to appreciate all the steps it took toward achieving your achievements by including your intentions, the details, and the time frames. The more you achieve, the greater your achievements become.

AFFIRMATION OF FOCUS

How many times do you hear the word focus? We all know what focus means and how important it is to achieve in life.

Affirmation

- Today and every day I will focus on my goals.
- The only way to succeed in life is to focus.
- Focus is my mental state of being.

FOCUS

As a parent, I recall telling my children to focus when it was time to do homework, or when I was dropping them off at school in the morning. I would say, "I love you. Stay focused."

Now here I am in my fifties reminding myself on a daily basis to focus to complete my to-do list or project with a deadline. It's easy to get distracted just by a simple thought that may cross our mind and take us off track for twenty to thirty minutes at a time.

I learned that having discipline is so important, if you want to become successful and achieve great things. If not, you will definitely be challenged. Developing the right tools and acquiring the right mindset is required to avoid distraction. I learned that putting a couple hours a day to the side to focus on projects will allow you to accomplish a lot in life. I believe finding that quiet time and space is definitely needed. The more you focus, the better you become great in what you want to achieve in life.

AFFIRMATION OF DETERMINATION

Determination is the objective of knowing your destination!
Once you know where you're going, nothing should get in
your way.

Affirmation

- I am determined to reach my goal.
- Determination is the key to life.
- I am determined to be great in my lifetime.

DETERMINATION

I can recall being a kid with no cares in the world. Having a mindset of focusing on something important didn't occur until I reached ten years old. I used to live across the street from a supermarket. Me and a couple of friends would get up early in the morning to bag groceries for the customers. This was my way of making money at a young age. We would take the groceries to the customer's cars, hoping to make money. It was my weekend hustle, and I would bring home twenty to thirty dollars a day. I was so determined, I got up early before the other children in the neighborhood so they wouldn't take my spot in the store.

Having that mindset at a young age gave me the advantage to apply to my adult life. I started setting goals when I was twenty-one years old. I wanted to become an office manager, own a house before I reached my thirty-fifth birthday, as well as start my own business as an entrepreneur.

When the recession took place in 2007-2008, I had the opportunity to start a finance business. I had saved enough to invest in a home. Due to the recession and some health issues, I changed my focus. As a result, my goals and determination had to be redirected. If you know anything about life, you know that life can shift you in another direction and take you off your course, causing you to develop a different mindset and mission. As we know, life experiences will often lead us in another direction that suits our purposes at the present time. Determination will always play a big role when we change focus and continue to make our goals a priority.

AFFIRMATION OF AMBITION

Having high standards to be what you want to be in life without letting anyone get in the way of your success is ambition. You learn to be true and honest about your dreams and what's important to you.

Affirmation

- I have the drive to achieve my dreams.
- It's my calling to be a great human being.
- I can do anything I put my mind to.

AMBITION

During life, we will come across certain times when the desire to do something becomes strong. The spark of interest may come from learning about something we've seen or heard someone say. That will light a fire inside of us to accomplish something. That's when ambition and drive kick in within us. There comes a certain force of energy that pushes us from within to meet the requirements and get it done.

Once you're able to align yourself and maintain that force of energy, you will be able to fully see the mission and the goal required. But nothing will happen until you're in full agreement with what you really want. It's knowing the why we push ourselves, the why we do certain things, the why we don't give up on trying something, that enables us to continue to be ambitious. It's all about the why we have, and the drive in us, that allows us to do anything. We must develop that understanding to succeed fully in life. Ambition is a force and drive that won't stop until we stop.

AFFIRMATION OF MOTIVATION

Once I put my mind and heart into wanting to do something, I'm motivated to get it done, no matter what it takes.

Affirmation

- I am excited and ready to achieve great things.
- I can do all things with the right mindset.
- I am unstoppable once I get started.

MOTIVATION

Sometimes in life we get stuck or stumble because of a life situation that will cause us to have a block that holds us back from moving forward. Many times, we really want to do something, but we don't have the resources or the knowledge of how to get started. Imagine you want to drive a car. It's the keys that you actually need to have in your hands. You begin to ask yourself, where do I start? Generally, it starts within self. We try to figure out how we can make this a reality. Often, fear plays a huge factor in holding us back. Why do we feel challenged to move forward? Most of the time, people worry about what other people may say about them or how they are perceived. So instead of dealing with all those emotions, people remain in their comfort zones. Until their comfort zones become uncomfortable, at which point they have to move on.

Now this is where it gets exciting. Once you begin to be forced to grab the keys because there is no other place to go, God will put you in a predicament that will turn your world upside down. That will make you have no other choice but to grab the keys and allow you to drive the car like you never drove before. This is what you call motivation. It will take you from one place in your life to a better place that you couldn't have ever imagined. Motivation always starts with you.

AFFIRMATION OF UNDERSTANDING

Having understanding is the most important principle in life. Without understanding life challenges, it becomes hard to determine the difference between lessons and what you must learn from the lessons.

Affirmation

- I am very knowledgeable about understanding life.
- I'm learning to become an understanding person.
- Understanding is a mindset that must be developed.

UNDERSTANDING

The greatest gift in life is having an understanding, so you have the capacity to process life situations and make sense of them. Without having the ability to comprehend life and its purpose, life will truly become unbearable to master at times. Therefore, you must understand how to handle obstacles and challenges, if you want to understand life. To learn to understand life, you must learn to understand yourself first. Understanding yourself allows you to see why certain life situations are happening to you. But first you must understand and agree that life happens for a reason, and there is no such thing as accidents. Things happen so you may understand what you must do in life so you can move forward into the next phase of your journey.

AFFIRMATION OF TRUST

Trust is such a powerful but crucial word that we as individuals must define the true meaning before applying it. I believe that trust is something that comes from within, such as our faith, belief, and confidence.

Affirmation

- I'm confident in my faith.
- I'm certain that my belief is all I need.
- I'm trusting that everything I do will be enough.

TRUST

Trusting in someone or something requires a lot of faith. I once heard someone say that we should trust everyone, because we all come from God, and there's a lesson in everything that we must learn. I agree with that statement wholeheartedly. But I must say, there's definitely a process with trust, regardless of who you decide is worthy of your trust.

The word trust is not a common word that is used frequently. Trust is often more of a demonstration of actions or behaviors that people show based on their relationships. This explains why some relationships don't last long. Now imagine if a relationship could last longer if we were taught to internalize trust towards ourselves, instead of holding others hostage with our expectations of our needs or wants. If you could imagine that and begin to expect nothing, only from yourself, then you can appreciate the value of building healthy relationships.

AFFIRMATION OF HONESTY

Being an honest individual says a lot about your character and who you are as an individual. Honesty doesn't show up easily, but when it does, learn from it. Honesty teaches you the essence of who you can be.

Affirmation

- I represent honesty when I walk.
- I stand alone in my honesty.
- Honesty builds up my character.

HONESTY

As we ponder the significance of the word honesty, we may not understand its importance or see the trace it leaves upon us. There are people who can read right through a person to determine if they are being honest by what they say or through their body language. I can recall in my younger years being challenged as I tried to determine who was being truthful and who was being dishonest. Until one day, I just started accepting whatever people said to be a true statement until it didn't match up with our next conversation. When things didn't line up, that would be a definite indication that the individual was untrustworthy. I wouldn't call them out or put them on the spot. Unfortunately, however, I would lose respect, because the values that they once carried no longer matched the values that I once held for them.

12

AFFIRMATION OF LOVE

Love is a word based on our feelings and emotions that many of us can't determine how to read. We can describe love, but we're still not sure what it really is when it hits us.

Affirmation

- I am loved and a loving human being.
- I am wrapped amongst the energy of love.
- I am constantly in the bliss of love and happiness.

LOVE

W e are told that love is a universal force of energy
that surrounds our natural being, fulfilling our
consciousness of despair and gratification of our true
essence. I don't believe we actually find love, but that love
finds us in the dark moments when we have given up
searching for the fulfillment that offers joy and happiness
that we have known.

We as individuals search for love that looks, sounds, and
feels familiar to our naked eye, without truly understanding
what we really need. It's not always about the present
moment, or who or what someone can do for you, and vice
versa, based on your vision. Love is something that's unseen.
Therefore, if you can see it, then you clearly can't understand it. But if you can feel it, and it brings balance to the
oneness of the true essence of what you believe love is
supposed to be, embrace it and the journey called love.

KEEP WALKING INTO YOUR PURPOSE

As we begin to walk into our purpose, we will stumble greatly along the way. We will find many resting places to stop and ponder about what caused us to stumble. The moment we begin to accept and release by exhaling, we will build ourselves up with words of uplifting affirmation while reaching toward our greatness.

If you enjoyed the book, please leave a review on any book platform. If you don't have time to leave a review, please rate with stars. Every star helps!

THANK YOU

I thank you for your loving support!

Stepping into the Spiritual World of your Greatness
www.charmaineholland.com

ABOUT THE AUTHOR

Charmaine Holland's passion and love for humanity will sweep you off your feet. She is an intuitive life coach, healer and speaker, whose powerful, uplifting guidance has changed the lives of people all over the world. For 30 years, Charmaine has taught people to seek their truth and live their best life by walking in their purpose and developing their true potential.

Charmaine has worked with great spiritual leaders among communities for more than 20 years, helping establish healthy foundations of love within families. She also visits and mentors women inside several California prisons.

Charmaine enjoys being an author, educator, financial advisor, and fashion designer. She is founder and president of four active businesses: Theloveofinspiringwomen.com, Ramadanjournal.com, CharmaineHolland.com, and Hollandsbookkeeping.com. She is the proud mother of two great young men and six grandkids. Her family continually inspires her to leave the next generation a better future.

www.ingramcontent.com/pod-product-compliance
Lightning Source LLC
Chambersburg PA
CBHW072041060426
42449CB00010BA/2382